WHISPERS OF A WITHERED HEART

SIDDHARTHA SINHA

Meant for someone whose identity is unknown yet important.

Contents

Part 1

Foreword

In the pages of Whispers of a Withered Heart, you will journey through the tangled emotions of love, loss, and the quiet echoes that linger long after the heart has been shattered. This collection offers a raw and unflinching look at the pain of an aching soul, walking a path of solitude and reflection. From the parched roads of despair to the glimmering mirages of hope, the poems explore the harsh realities of life's trials while never fully relinquishing the desire for healing.

Each verse carries with it the weight of personal experience—each word carefully chosen to convey a heart battered by its own desires and disappointments. As the poet navigates through feelings of longing, regret, and the struggle to move on, they invite the reader to sit with them in their sorrow and to find, amid the pain, the quiet resilience that comes from facing the darkness.

The collection's title, Whispers of a Withered Heart, speaks to the quiet suffering that often goes unnoticed by the world, and yet, in its softest moments, reveals a truth—brokenness is not the end. It is a part of the journey, a step toward rediscovery, even if the path forward is unclear.

...

These poems are a testament to the human experience, a reflection of the raw vulnerability we all share when confronted by love's fragility. They serve as a reminder that while hearts may wither, they also have the capacity to grow, to heal, and to endure. For those who have loved deeply, lost painfully, and sought meaning in the wreckage of it all, this book is for you.

Welcome to a world of whispered sorrows, fleeting moments of hope, and the quiet strength found in the midst of heartache. Whispers of a Withered Heart is not just a collection of poems—it is a journey toward understanding and, perhaps, even reconciliation with the deepest parts of ourselves.

• viii •

Preface

Whispers of a Withered Heart began as a quiet collection of thoughts—raw, unfiltered, and deeply personal. It grew over time as an exploration of the delicate threads that bind us to the emotions we often struggle to understand: love, longing, loss, and the spaces between. In these pages, you will encounter poems that were born from moments of silence, from the pain of unspoken words, and from the desperate search for solace in the aftermath of heartache.

The journey to create this collection was not one of smooth transitions or neat resolutions. Instead, it was a winding road through a desert of emotions, where each poem became a stepping stone on a path that sometimes felt too heavy to walk. But as with all journeys of the heart, the beauty lies not in the destination, but in the act of moving through the pain and the discovery of resilience in the most unexpected places.

Each poem in this book captures a different facet of love's complexities—its ability to elevate us to the heights of joy, and its power to tear us apart, leaving us questioning ourselves and our worth. The imagery of a withered heart is not meant to convey hopelessness, but rather the quiet truth that from the deepest wounds, new growth can emerge. It is through the cracks and the scars that we often find our greatest strength.

Writing these poems was a form of catharsis, a way of reaching out into the void for answers that may never come, and yet still clinging to the idea that healing is possible. They reflect a constant dance between despair and hope, between the desire to retreat from the world and the push to keep moving forward.

This collection is not just for those who have experienced the sharp pangs of loss, but for anyone who has ever questioned the meaning of love, the nature of pain, or the possibility of renewal. It is for the ones who have stood on the edge of their own despair, only to find that something, however small, still flickers within them.

If you pick up this book, I ask you to read with an open heart, to sit with the discomfort that these words may stir, and to find comfort in knowing that you are not alone. There is a quiet beauty in the brokenness, a whispering strength in the vulnerability, and a reminder that even a withered heart can still feel, still hope, and still grow.

Thank you for walking this path with me.

1. If I Were A Tree

In the depths of the forest,
Far from sight or sound,
A tree crushed into the ground,
Ending its life with the earth's embrace.
Yet when I'm at my lowest,
You won't even hug me?
I really wish I was a tree.

2. Desert of the Soul

The parched road that takes me
To this dry wasteland that conspires
To breach my forsaken soul and mislead
Each agonizing step is set on fire

I breathe the deep still air
That quiets my scorched heart
As my heated passion flares
drawing out the salty sorrow it imparts

This arid sweat of memories entreat
Love's mirage that solemnly passes
On distant rims appear to char with fiery heat
From desert winds that carry disappearing ashes

3. Frozen in Time

my heart is here while yours is away
forever in this realm am I to stay
There are so many words I must say
no more How do you do or love you too
just the morning laced with blue dew

today I saw the flower of our love
in the showers of feathers from a dove
like snow in the sun they glistened
hearing your voice every word I listened
it seemed as if this moment was that of a dream
sugar laced tears fell from my face
how I wished we could both be in the same place
being graced by your touch embraced by your smell
since you left my world has been a living hell
I'm just a shell of a man reverting to a boy
but the feeling of your spiritual presence
brings me joy
remembering those words you spoke so wise
to always look up to the skies to find
the star that shines bright
That is how I know you there at night
and during the day embrace the sun's ray
That's your touch but

bittersweet i lay in our love garden
feeling my skin start to harden
I've become a statue frozen in time
waiting for the day your lips meet mine

4. Faded

i've spent too much time, feeling lost inside
It was black, it was gray
I still dream of the day that I could believe, "I promise you I won't leave"

But what am I supposed to do, when no one can follow through?
Is this all love will ever be?
Broken promises, and faded memories?

I don't want it to be this way
I'm losing my mind more every day
Yeah, you promised that you would stay
How come everyone just leaves?
Is there something wrong with me?

When I love you turns to dust
Hell, there's no one I can trust
Slowly the walls of our love crumble down
And I just lay there trapped beneath the ground

Will someone ever pulled me out?
If only I could live without
I'm tired of the same old love
Someday I hope that I can float above

i want to soar above this pain
But i've learned that love's a losing game
Can't pretend that i don't care
The way you broke me wasn't fair

5. Shattered Shield

There's no cure for a broken heart
There's No fix or button to press restart
So I lie here in my bed falling apart

I just wish I could rewind to you and me
But some things just aren't meant to be
And some chains you just can't break free

The chains of heartbreak weigh on my soul
Where my heart should be there's only a hole
Gaping as dark as night and as black as coal

And people tell me time can heal any pain
But I'm not sure, I just want to see you again
Because maybe then I'd be able to explain

the ways I loved you but couldn't show
So please I'm begging you not to go
Because if you do you'll never know

All the ways losing you tore at my mind
Turning it into a monster no longer kind
the connection of heart and soul untwined

Two separate pieces that lay under my skin
The line between insanity and reality grows thin
It's like hiding inside my mind there's a twin

A version of who I used to be, of who I was some time ago
And a version me who hides how they feel so they'll never show
That given time their pain and sorrow will only ever grow

So no, not all wounds will heal if given the time
I need a helping hand to help me make that climb
someone who understands the words in my rhyme

Someone who can understand the pain when a heart breaks in two
Someone who can help me understand whatever it is I need to do
To help me heal and mend my broken heart, someone to get me through

But I still see you in my sleep, see nightmares of you leaving when I dream
Every dream I have carries the same person, a repeated neverending theme
I wake up with a gasp sometimes with a shout pleading as tears stream

Now I blame myself for everything as my self-confidence starts to crack
Saying I'm okay as the weight of all our memories once happy start to
stack
On top of each other but instead of rainbows they stain my soul black

Because they only remind me of what's no longer here
I still find it hard to believe it's nearly been a year
Now grief and sorrow take hold and my eyes tear

And I try to think of you happy, I try my best to miss you less
And on some days it looks like it helps, like I make progress
But then suddenly anxiety takes hold and I'm just a mess

So I've given up on being brave in the battlefield
I have already raised the white flag and tried to yield
But you're not here to be my bright shining shield

But you're not here to shield me from my brain
Taunting me with all the memories that remain
You were the shield that had kept me sane

6. Don't Ask Why

Love's ecstasy flew on gilded wings
To this heart laden with woe;
Like the buds of Spring my dreams unfurled...
And then Fate dealt its cruel blow.
Now I walk that lonely path again,
But I'll forget her... just don't ask when

How does a shattered heart find its way,
Deprived of its guiding star?
How long will it take before it heals?
Do wounds this deep leave a scar?
Though my world is crumbling 'round me now,
I must carry on... just don't ask how

Trying to hush echoes of the past,
Alone I bitterly weep;
I've climbed the Hill of Sorrows before ...
But it's never been this steep!
Each day dark clouds are filling my sky,
And yet, I still hope... just don't ask why

But should abandoned hearts dare to hope
Lost love will return again?
Last night as I prayed I thought I heard

Crying angels sighing Amen;
Now I bravely flaunt this smiling mask,
But do I still miss her?... Please, don't ask!

7. Ephemeral Magic

You begat the life in me
blackened numb, you found the light
a piece of clay you molded
into platinum satellites

I drifted through your eyes of blue
you put the "u" in us
helped to get me back onboard
when I fell off the bus

your body was my road map
as I trudged your steep terrain
drowning in your sea supplied me
room to breathe again

that planet filled with stars and moons
the rock on which I stood
then vanished like a whisp of smoke
as magic only could.

8. Eternal Whispers

When the wind blows then
you may hear me.

Or as leaves rustle in the trees.

When mist rises in the morning
you may see me.

Or when the song is free.

When the sun rises in the dawning
you will then know my smile.

In evening I am with you all the while.

When you need someone to listen
without talking, I am there.

We are forever and know that I still care.

9. Lost to the Sky

Like a spark lost in flames
A single tear washed in rain
A meter meandering in a poem
A drop drowning in the ocean

Like a star blinded by the sun
Like our every kiss overdone
Like my passion unfed, unburnt
Like your love still unconcerned

A child unearthing simple treasures
A boy apeing shadow's pleasures
My regret to dive without measure
My guilt to not let me surrender

To let it rot and to see it unfoil
Or get bitter, to unmake and destroy
No end sought would lead to joy
No choice remains a right choice

I lost to the guile, gaining nigh
I skipped a lark to catch a fly
In a moment, have lost her to the sky
Our love will be saved, but will I?

10. Timeless Redemption

If things could be quite faultless; seamless and divine.
Id fervently erase missteps; all of yours, and mine.
Never a depression day, nevermore dysfunction
When issues do arise we face and conquer them, with gumption.
A thousand sunsets we'd observe, our bodies snug and close.
A gentle smile would curve your lips; you'd never feel morose.
If I could just go back and change, make everything brand new,
I would still give you my all, and Id still be everything to you.

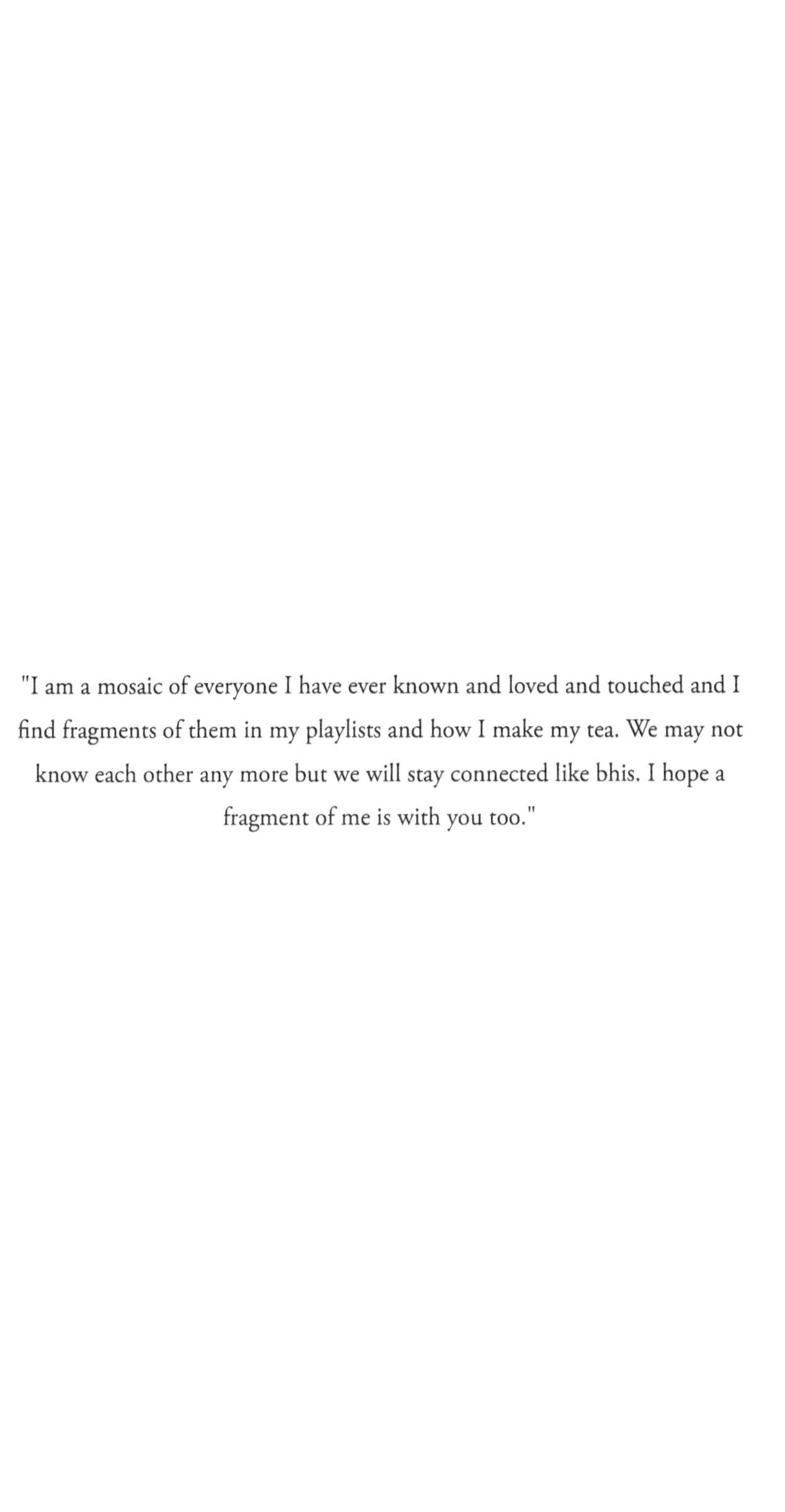

"I am a mosaic of everyone I have ever known and loved and touched and I find fragments of them in my playlists and how I make my tea. We may not know each other any more but we will stay connected like bhis. I hope a fragment of me is with you too."